Modern methods of house construction
A surveyor's guide

Keith Ross

BRE Construction Division

bretrust

The information in this publication is still correct, it may be out of date or BRE no longer have
the expertise to support it. The BRE Group and IHS Markit do not accept any responsibility for
any subsequent use of this publication, nor for any errors or omissions they may contain.

This work has been funded by BRE Trust. Any views expressed are not necessarily those of BRE Trust. While every effort is made to ensure the accuracy and quality of information and guidance when it is first published, BRE Trust can take no responsibility for the subsequent use of this information, nor for any errors or omissions it may contain.

The mission of BRE Trust is 'Through education and research to promote and support excellence and innovation in the built environment for the benefit of all'. Through its research programmes the Trust aims to achieve:
● a higher quality built environment
● built facilities that offer improved functionality and value for money
● a more efficient and sustainable construction sector, with
● a higher level of innovative practice.

A further aim of the Trust is to stimulate debate on challenges and opportunities in the built environment.

BRE Trust
Garston, Watford, Herts WD25 9XX
Tel: 01923 664598
Email: secretary@bretrust.co.uk
www.bretrust.org.uk

BRE Trust and BRE publications are available from:
www.brebookshop.com
or
IHS Rapidoc (BRE Bookshop)
Willoughby Road
Bracknell RG12 8DW
Tel: 01344 404407
Fax: 01344 714440
Email: brebookshop@ihsrapidoc.com

Published by BRE Bookshop for BRE Trust

Requests to copy any part of this publication
should be made to:
BRE Bookshop
Garston, Watford, Herts WD25 9XX
Tel: 01923 664761
Email: brebookshop@emap.com

FB11
© Copyright BRE Trust 2005
First published 2005
ISBN 1 86081 755 6

Preface

Pressure from Government to increase the rate of housing supply, a diminishing skills base and higher performance requirements for dwellings have resulted in the introduction of a wide range of innovative components and construction systems into house construction.

The planning system, on the other hand, has remained conservative and, in general, has restricted the introduction of visually different finishes to the exterior of dwellings. The result has been that, while builders have begun to introduce innovative components and systems into their product, they have at the same time been required to make the resulting dwellings resemble conventional construction as closely as possible.

As more and more dwellings are built using these modern methods of construction, surveyors will increasingly find themselves being required to assess dwellings of markedly different construction to the conventional masonry structures they are used to. The purpose of this guide is to introduce surveyors to the range of constructions currently being used, thereby enabling them to produce more meaningful and informed reports for their clients.

KR
2005

Acknowledgements

I would like to express my profound thanks to the following individuals and organisations for their invaluable support and guidance during the preparation of this guide.

Jim Baker	The Forge Company
Jackie Bennett	Council of Mortgage Lenders
Roger Courtney	Formerly BRE
Mark Gorgolowski	Steel Construction Institute
Harry Harrison	Formerly BRE
Kim Mathen	Peabody Trust (now with Mark 1 Associates)
Martin Milner	TRADA (now with Chiltern Clarke Bond)
Fran Nowak	Formerly BRE
Malcolm Potter	Davis Langdon
Chris Watts	Housing Corporation (now with Beyond Green)
Nick Whitehouse	Terrapin International Ltd

I would also like to thank the many organisations who have given permission to reproduce images.

Contents

Introduction   1

Modern methods of construction   **5**
  Volumetric construction   6
  Panellised systems   9
    Steel panels   10
    Timber panels   12
    Concrete panels   12
    Structural Insulated Panels (SIPs)   14
    Composite panels   15
  Hybrid construction   17
  Sub-assemblies and components   18
    Floor construction   18
    Roof construction   21
  Site-based modern methods of construction   22
    Tunnelform   22
    Aircrete (aerated concrete) products   23
  Other innovations in traditional materials and techniques   25
    Insulating concrete formwork   25
    Brick slips   26

Distinguishing between traditional and modern methods of construction on site   **29**
  External inspection   30
    Brick finish   30
    Rendered finish   41
  Internal inspection   45
    Internal walls   45
    Floors   49
  Loft and roof structure   52
    Gable and party walls   52
    Roof trusses   52
    Lofts suitable for habitation (room-in-the-roof)   53

Site checklist   **55**

Further reading   **60**

Introduction

The aim of this guide is to provide surveyors with an insight into how to differentiate between houses built using modern methods of construction (MMC) and those built using more 'traditional' site-based techniques such as brick and block cavity construction. There is, though, no precise definition of what constitutes a modern method of construction. A simple definition might be:

'dwellings whose structural units are wholly or in part manufactured off site, or on site by contemporary methods other than 'traditional' methods such as brick and block cavity masonry'.

The definition also needs to include some reference to date; only recent systems (eg from the mid 1990s) are regarded as 'modern methods'. Earlier manufactured systems are normally referred to as 'non-traditional'. More is said in Box 1 about the difficulty of defining modern methods of construction.

Many of the so-called non-traditional systems produced housing that looks markedly different from masonry construction: this immediately alerts the surveyor to the fact that the dwelling is not of masonry construction (Figure 1). However, many of the modern systems are designed to look like 'traditional' houses and thus, from the street, do not appear to be anything other than conventional houses (Figure 2).

This guide is divided into 2 main parts, providing:

- an overview of the principal forms of housing constructed by modern methods to demonstrate the fundamental differences between these methods of construction and those expected to be used on a block and brick cavity based building;
- specific examples of the visual clues that can help the surveyor to recognise what form of construction has been used.

Box 1 'Modern' or 'Non-traditional'?

The difficulty of defining what constitutes a 'modern' method of construction (rather than 'non-traditional') can be illustrated by taking timber-frame construction as an example.

Timber-frame dwellings (other than early forms such as Tudor post and beam) were introduced as early as 1920 and dozens of new systems were developed in the 1960s. These early timber-frame systems are usually referred to as 'non-traditional'.

Since the 1980s, timber-frame construction has been referred to as just that, 'timber-frame', and has largely been in the form of factory-made panels delivered to site for assembly. The panels typically comprise a studwork frame with pre-formed openings for windows and doors, and with a plywood or other sheathing material fitted. All assembly and other works (external cladding, installation of insulation, fitting of windows, internal lining board, services, etc.) is undertaken on site.

In more recent years much of this work, and in some cases assembly into three-dimensional units (ie volumetric construction), has been undertaken in the factory. These systems might be included within the definition of 'modern methods of construction'. However, volumetric construction has also been in use for a number of years. For example, Calder houses were of volumetric timber construction and were first introduced in the 1960s. Because of their age they are referred to as 'non-traditional' rather than 'modern'.

The term 'modern methods of construction' also covers site-based systems other than masonry cavity construction, such as thin joint blockwork, cast-in-situ concrete (eg Tunnelform) or aircrete planks. Again, referring to these systems as 'modern' is a misnomer since many of the systems have been in use in other countries for up to 30 years. They have been included in this guide because they are relatively new to the UK.

The examples discussed refer to housing constructed using modern (rather than 'non-traditional') forms of construction. This guide does not discuss the advantages or disadvantages of the various methods of construction, a summary of which can be found in BRE's *Good Building Guide 56*.

Figure 1
Nissen–Petren 'non-traditional' housing

Figure 2
An example of a 'modern' factory-built house

For guidance on older forms of non-traditional housing, refer to *Non-traditional houses* (Harrison et al 2004), a major reference work to over 450 non-traditional systems built between 1918 and 1975 that provides a detailed catalogue of metal-framed, in-situ and precast concrete, and timber-framed houses. In addition, a series of reports produced by BRE on individual systems are listed in *Further reading* at the end of this guide.

Modern methods of construction

The term 'modern methods of construction' covers a broad range of construction types ranging from complete housing systems built in factories through to new site-based technologies. Older terms such as 'system building', 'off-site assembly', 'industrialised construction' and 'modular construction' are still used by many. A simple classification of modern methods by built form is:

- Volumetric construction,
- Panellised systems,
- Hybrid construction,
- Sub-assemblies and components,
- Site-based methods of construction.

The first four categories are usually manufactured in a factory; the term 'site-based methods' covers systems that do not fall neatly into the first four categories. This first part of the guide describes the form and nature of these construction types to provide background knowledge that will aid the identification process.

Volumetric construction

Volumetric construction involves the production of three-dimensional units in a factory (Figure 3). The units are transported to site where they are stacked onto prepared foundations to form the dwellings (Figure 4). A typical house is made from four units, whereas flats might comprise one or (more usually) two units depending on size.

Figure 3
Volumetric modules being assembled in a factory

Figure 4
Volumetric unit being positioned on foundations

All the necessary internal finishes, services and, potentially, the furnishings can be installed at the factory, with the complete entity able to be transported to site and assembled. Some external finishes can also be factory fitted, but usually some work has to be done on site in order to make good the join between units.

To date most volumetric construction has been in the hotel, student and key-worker accommodation, health care and fast food sectors, where repetition of built form (either at the building level, or at the room level) is common. However, this method of construction is also now being used for housing. Figure 5 shows a prototype pair of semi-detached dwellings manufactured by Britspace. Each dwelling comprises four volumetric modules plus panellised roof.

Volumetric units can also be added to existing buildings to create new facilities.

A particular feature of volumetric construction is that, in allowing the units to be transported and craned into position without being damaged, they need to be strengthened sufficiently to increase their rigidity. In some instances, temporary bracing is attached to the modules for transportation, but in other cases, additional or larger members are incorporated into the structure, effectively making the units stronger than they need to be for in-service requirements.

Figure 5
Prototype volumetric dwellings by Britspace

Volumetric construction can be in almost any material. Examples are known in steel, timber and concrete. If the frames are made of steel they are usually cold-rolled, light gauge galvanised C sections with a typical thickness range of 1–3.2 mm. In domestic properties, the whole structure can be made using light gauge cold-rolled steel. However, some manufacturers use thicker hot-rolled sections for corner posts and edge beams to give the extra strength required for transportation and lifting.

Due to the physical limitations of road transport, volumetric units are usually less than 4 m in width and, although unit lengths of 16 m are possible, lengths within the range of 8–12 m are more typical.

Figure 6 shows modular units being assembled on-site. In this example, the external finish is of brick slips, most of which have been factory-fitted. A conventional 100 mm brick outer leaf could have been built on site after the modules had been stacked as an alternative to brick slips.

Figure 6
Volumetric units being stacked on site (Courtesy of Guinness Trust)

Panellised systems

Flat panel units are produced in a factory (Figure 7) using purpose-made jigs or machinery to ensure dimensional accuracy and are transported to site for assembly. Panels can be of a variety of materials and constructions, ranging from framed panels in either timber or steel, to concrete and composite panels such as SIPs (structural insulated panels). Framed panels can be of two basic types: 'open' or 'closed'. The meaning of these terms has changed over time. During the period that non-traditional housing was being constructed, an 'open' system was one that could accept components from any source, whereas a 'closed' system was one that could accept components from only a few sources that produced components specific to the system. In the context of modern methods of construction, the terms have the following interpretations.

- **Open panel system**
  This is a framing system (metal or timber) delivered to site before insulation, services, etc. are fitted.
- **Closed panel system**
  This is a complex panel system that can have services, windows, doors, internal wall finishes and external claddings fitted at the factory.

Figure 7
A factory manufacturing panels (Courtesy of Space4)

Steel panels

Steel-framed panels are most commonly 'open' and do not include insulation, lining boards, etc. Such panels are also referred to as 'sub-frames'. Insulation to external walls is normally applied to the outside of the frame on site (although it can be factory-installed), sometimes supplemented by more insulation between the studs (Figure 8).

The practice of fixing insulation to the external face of the frame creates a 'warm frame' construction that is very effective at reducing thermal bridging across steel members and also allows services to be installed between the steel studs. Figure 9 shows a typical panellised steel frame building during construction.

Steel panels are also now being fabricated on site using 'portable factories'. These facilities take rolls of galvanised steel stock and extrude the profiles required to make the panel on site. The rolling machines are quite sophisticated in that they can be programmed to cut the sections to length and pre-punch holes for rivets and other fixings very accurately. This means

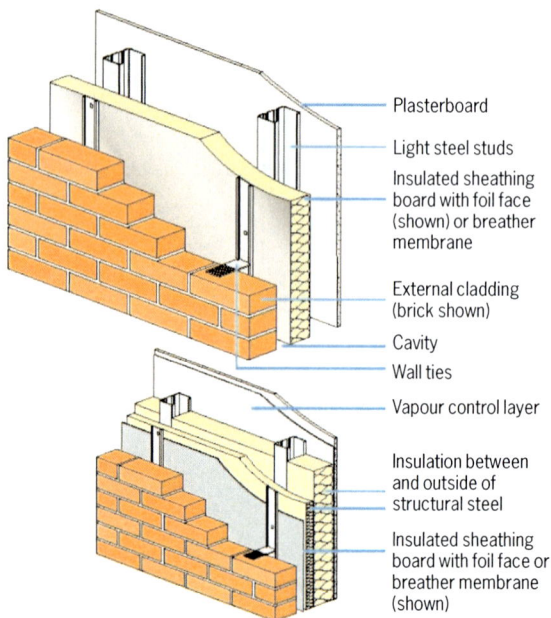

Plasterboard

Light steel studs

Insulated sheathing board with foil face (shown) or breather membrane

External cladding (brick shown)

Cavity

Wall ties

Vapour control layer

Insulation between and outside of structural steel

Insulated sheathing board with foil face or breather membrane (shown)

Figure 8

Typical steel-frame constructions
© Crown copyright reproduced from *Limiting thermal bridging and air leakage: robust construction details for dwellings and similar buildings* with the permission of the Controller of HMSO and Queen's Printer for Scotland

that the resulting panels are dimensionally more accurate than those produced on site using 'stick' construction (ie where the building is constructed from lengths of stock material and accuracy depends on the skill of the fabricator). Figure 10 shows a typical site-based rolling mill, Figure 11 shows a panel produced from it.

Figure 9
Panellised steel-framed building being erected

Figure 10
Portable rolling mill

Figure 11
Typical steel-framed panel from a portable mill

Timber panels

'Conventional' timber-frame panels normally arrive on site with sheathing board fixed but with no insulation, etc. With modern systems insulation, service conduits, linings and window frames can all be factory-fitted. Figure 12 shows one example of modern timber-framed construction. However, in the finished building it can be difficult distinguishing between 'modern' and conventional timber frames.

Figure 12
Modern timber-frame construction: note the factory-fitted window frame (Courtesy of Space4)

Concrete panels

Large concrete panels have been used since the 1950s in non-traditional construction, especially in flats and high-rise construction. Panels are usually two-dimensional, but can be more complicated. Figure 13 shows a house being built in Finland with flat concrete panels, whereas Figure 14 shows a system based on 'L'-shaped panels.

More sophisticated concrete panels are also being produced that incorporate factory-fitted cladding and windows. Figure 15 shows the manufacture of one such system that incorporates cladding of bricks cut lengthways to simulate a brick wall of stretcher bond.

Figure 13
House being
constructed using
flat concrete panels

Figure 14
Housing system
based on L-shaped
concrete panels
(Courtesy of Brycon)

Figure 15
Manufacture of brick-
faced concrete
panels (Courtesy of
Milbank)

Structural Insulated Panels (SIPs)

SIPs are essentially a sandwich construction comprising two layers of sheet material bonded to a foam insulation core. They have no internal studs within the panels and rely on the bond between the foam and the two layers of sheet material to form a load-bearing unit (though there may be studs at corners and around some openings). SIP panels are used in the same way as timber- or steel-framed panels. One advantage of SIP panels is that the insulation layer is more continuous than in normal framed panels. This leads to better thermal performance for a given thickness of panel because of the absence of thermal bridges associated with studs. In the US where SIP construction has been used for a number of years, panels vary in thickness from 100 mm to around 300 mm.

The two layers of sheet material can be of a variety of materials; oriented strand board and cement-based boards are fairly common. The rigid foam core will usually be expanded polystyrene, polyurethane or polyisocyanurate. Figure 16 shows a close-up of a SIP showing the construction and one method of joining adjacent panels. Figure 17 shows a house being built using SIPs. Various devices, such as special cramps for use during assembly or cam-lock fittings built into the panels, are used to pull the panels together to assist with creating an airtight join.

A BRE *Information Paper* (IP13/04) gives an introduction to building with SIPs.

Figure 16
Close-up of a SIP panel (Courtesy of Kingspan Tek)

Figure 17
A house being constructed using SIPs (Courtesy of Kingspan Tek)

Composite panels

There are a number of modern systems that produce walls of composite construction (strictly speaking, any panel that is made from a combination of different materials is a composite panel, though most are not referred to as such). Some, such as insulating formwork, are site-based methods (see section on *Site-based modern methods of construction*), whereas others are factory-made panels. Some older, non-traditional, large panel systems were composites in that a layer of insulation was sandwiched between two layers of concrete (these would not be classified as SIPs because the structural load was borne by the relatively massive inner concrete layer). One type of 'modern' composite system has a foam insulation core within a wire space frame, all of which is encased in fine aggregate concrete. The systems range from:

● flat reinforced insulation panels that are erected and a render finish applied on site, to:
● a system that comprises a number of standard panels along with a system of connecting brackets and channels to facilitate accurate assembly on site, illustrated in Figure 18.

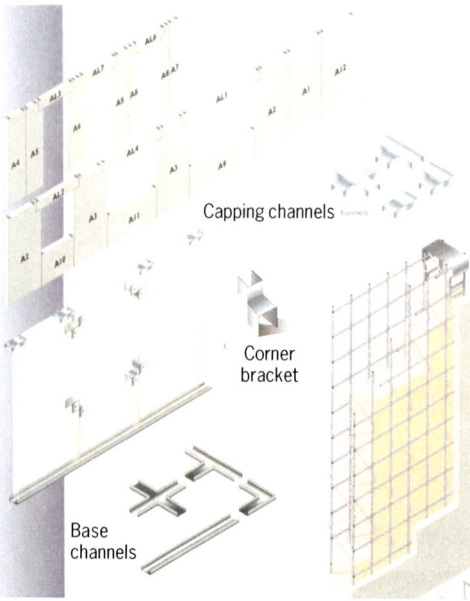

Capping channels

Corner bracket

Base channels

Figure 18
Composite panel system (Courtesy of Structherm)

Hybrid construction

This method of construction is also known as semi-volumetric as it combines both volumetric and panellised approaches within the same building (Figure 19). Volumetric units can be used for the highly serviced areas such as kitchens and bathrooms, with the remainder of the dwelling being constructed with panels. Examples of hybrid construction have been built in a variety of materials, and it is feasible to use different construction materials for the different parts. For example, steel-frame can be used for the volumetric element and timber-frame for the panellised element. However, in such circumstances, care is needed in the design to cater for differences in thermal and moisture movements of the different materials.

Figure 19
Hybrid construction: volumetric unit being positioned alongside panels

Sub-assemblies and components

This section covers items that are not full 'systems', but which use factory-made components either within manufactured dwellings or within otherwise traditionally built dwellings. Components such as door sets, windows, stair strings and other manufactured components are commonly used in all forms of construction and therefore do not fall within the definition of modern methods of construction. The main items relevant to this guide are innovative floor and roof constructions and modern composite joists.

Floor construction

A number of innovations have been introduced in flooring technology for houses. Solid timber joists are being replaced by engineered products such as timber I beams and lattice joists that are lighter and stiffer than solid timber. Joists up to ~ 0.5 m deep and up to 12 m long can be produced that are both lightweight and rigid, making it practical to span much larger distances without the need for intermediate structural support. Also, because of the relatively open structure that can be achieved, it is much easier to accommodate services within the floor as illustrated in Figures 20 and 21.

Floor cassettes are prefabricated framed units that are delivered to site ready-assembled in the same way as wall panels. Openings for stair wells will normally be formed in the factory. The joists can be of timber, light gauge steel or a composite. Figure 22 shows a light gauge steel floor cassette being installed.

The cassettes can be designed for long spans that require no support other than around the perimeter (thus allowing open-plan accommodation to be produced), so may be much thicker than normal floors.

Figure 20
The use of deep timber I beams gives long spans and easy accommodation of services within the depth of the floor (Courtesy of Excel Industries Ltd)

Figure 21
Steel web lattice joists

Floor cassettes can vary in the complexity of construction, ranging from simple box construction to systems designed for specific purposes such as separating floors with good acoustic properties. Figure 23 illustrates a floor cassette designed specifically for good acoustic performance.

Figure 22
Steel-framed floor cassette being lowered into position (Courtesy of The Forge Company)

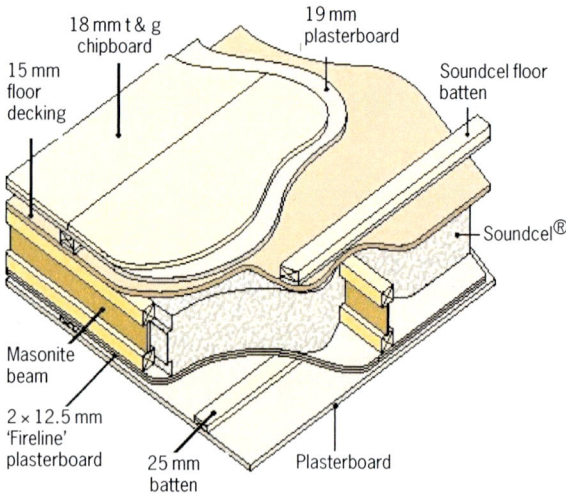

Figure 23
'Soundcel' flooring system (Courtesy of Excel Industries Ltd)

Roof construction

Products and components for roof construction are very similar to those for floor construction. The main difference is the need to incorporate thermal insulation. Roof cassettes comprise panels that span from eaves to ridge. They often require no intermediate structural support, although in some cases purlins are used. A range of designs and materials is employed. The panels may be of SIP-type construction or have internal studs, and panels can be hinged at the ridge. Both faces of the panels are normally finished with a sheet material, and insulation is included within the structure of the panel. Tiling battens can also be factory-fitted. Roof panels are useful for room-in-the-roof constructions where the absence of structural timbers is beneficial. Figure 24 shows roof cassette panels being installed.

Figure 24
Prefabricated roof cassettes being installed (Courtesy of Milbank)

Site-based modern methods of construction

This section relates to site-based assembly methods and the use of traditional components in an innovative way. Examples of construction forms that are generally accepted as 'modern methods of construction' are Tunnelform (cast-in-situ concrete using heated steel moulds), aircrete planks and thin joint blockwork. The next section describes other innovations in 'traditional' materials and techniques. These include the use of brick slips, insulating formwork and single-leaf masonry. These methods can be mixed with other forms of construction.

Tunnelform

Tunnelform construction is by no means new and has been used extensively in Holland and other parts of Europe for over 20 years. A substantial proportion of residential buildings are still built there using Tunnelform.

In this form of construction, 'L'-shaped steel shutters are used to cast concrete 'tunnels'. The moulds are heated overnight to accelerate the cure of the concrete and allow the moulds to be removed and re-used on a 24-hour cycle. Reinforcement and service conduits can be placed within the moulds as necessary before pouring the concrete, and openings for stair wells and interconnecting doors can also be formed. The resulting structure is a series of open-ended bays (Figure 25) with concrete walls and ceilings. The open ends of the bays are closed with a different system, often a panel system, but could be anything including cavity masonry in a similar way to more conventional cross-wall construction. The bays can be sub-divided internally to make more than one room.

Figure 25
Open-ended bays
formed by
Tunnelform

Aircrete (aerated concrete) products

There are two types of product that have recently been introduced into UK
house building, namely thin joint blockwork and aerated concrete planks
(although aircrete planks were used in at least one non-traditional system
during the 1960s). As the name implies, thin joint blockwork is constructed
using a thin (approx. 4 mm) bed of special mortar. The mortar is mixed on
site with a standard plasterer's whisk attachment in an electric drill to
produce a smooth, free-flowing adhesive. The blocks are larger than normal
blocks, and are dimensionally more accurate. Figure 26 illustrates thin layer
mortar masonry in use. More information on thin layer mortar masonry can
be found in BRE's *Good Building Guide 58*.

Figure 26
Thin layer mortar
being applied to
aircrete blocks.
Courtesy of H+H
Celcon

Thin joint blockwork can be used as a direct substitute for conventional blockwork or in conjunction with aerated concrete planks, ie large reinforced planks of aerated concrete up to approx. 6 m in length, in a range of widths (up to approx. 600 mm) and thicknesses (200–300 mm). The planks can be used to form floor and roof elements of buildings. When used in conjunction with aircrete blockwork the whole structural envelope is made of aircrete. Figure 27 shows the inside of a house being constructed with aircrete products. The external walls are of thin joint blockwork, internal walls are of large thin joint blockwork, and floors and roof are of aerated concrete plank construction.

Figure 27
House using aerated concrete products for all major elements

Other innovations in traditional materials and techniques

Insulating concrete formwork

Insulating concrete formwork derives its name from the fact that an insulation material (usually expanded polystyrene) is used as permanent shuttering for a cast-in-situ structural concrete wall. A number of systems exist, some of which are based on two sheets of insulating material tied together, whereas others are in the form of large hollow building blocks.

This type of construction has been popular in the self-build sector because of the ease with which an energy-efficient, airtight construction can be produced with minimal construction skills being required on the part of the self-builder, and because the mould materials are easily man-handled without the need for lifting equipment. Reinforcement can be introduced locally to add strength, for example over openings to create integral lintels as the concrete is poured. Figures 28 and 29 show insulating formwork buildings under construction. More information can be found at www.icfinfo.org.uk.

Figure 28
Insulating formwork before filling with concrete

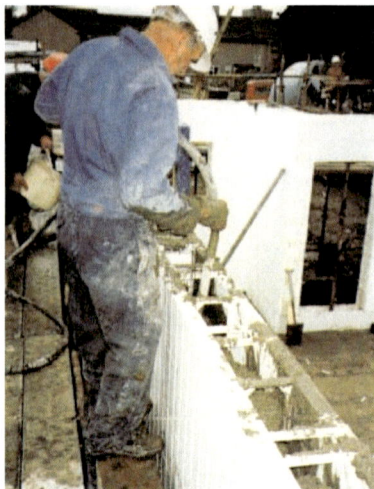

Figure 29
Insulating formwork: concrete being compacted with vibrating poker

Brick slips

An increasingly common feature of off-site manufactured housing is the use of brick slips that have been fixed in panels on the external walls of the property to give the appearance of a 'traditional' brick outer leaf. Brick slips are produced in two main ways, either by cutting the faces off a normal brick (each brick yielding up to two brick slips) or by extrusion (ie the wet clay is pressed through a die and cut using wire in the same way that wire cut bricks are produced). The slips vary in thickness according to the manufacturer, but 15–20 mm would be typical. L-shaped slips are produced for corner details. Figure 30 shows a number of 'standard' profiles.

Figure 30
Examples of brick slips

The slips are usually adhesively bonded to a substrate that can be either some form of backing sheet (eg a galvanised steel sheet with a pvc coating) or a profiled rigid foam that also provides the thermal insulation to the structure (Figure 31). Figure 32 shows another system where a profiled extruded brick slip is clipped into a metal profile and therefore does not rely on an adhesive bond to retain the slip. Because of the unique profile of the brick slips in this system they are somewhat thicker than other slips and corner slips are produced by a bonded mitre joint.

The use of brick slips is a strong indicator that the property is manufactured, but the absence of a brick slip system does not necessarily mean that the property is of traditional construction. Any manufactured system can accept a 100 mm brick outer leaf.

Figure 31
Brick slips bonded to polystyrene insulation before pointing

Figure 32
Brick slip system designed for mechanical fixing

Distinguishing between traditional and modern methods of construction on site

The intention of many contemporary house builders using modern methods of construction is to produce buildings that appear similar to those that have been constructed in brick and block cavity masonry. From a casual drive by of a property you may think that it is something it is not. Closer inspection of the property helped by a checklist of inspection clues will determine the construction methodology used to build it, without the need for intrusive or destructive examination.

This second part of the guide details a number of clues that should help determine whether or not a house has been constructed, if only partially, using modern methods. As with any form of construction, a single attribute may point to a number of possible answers but a combination of different clues will enable a picture of the property to be built up so that the number of possibilities can be narrowed down.

Inspection of the outside of the building is considered in the first section and internal inspection in the second section.

External inspection

As with traditional construction, the exterior of manufactured dwellings can have a wide variety of finishes, usually brick, render, hanging tile or timber boards. From the outside of a building, tile hung and timber boarded facades look no different on manufactured and conventional buildings so will not be discussed further.

Brick finish

The main question when faced with a brick finish is whether the wall has a 100 mm brick outer leaf or some form of brick slip finish. The following list of items should be considered when inspecting the brickwork to determine whether or not the façade you are looking at is constructed of brickwork or slip bricks.

- Weep holes
- Detailing around openings
- Regularity of brickwork (especially perpends)
- Mortar and brickwork colour banding
- Damp-proof courses
- Thickness of the external wall
- Structural considerations

Weep holes
The absence of weep holes indicates either no cavity or bad practice. If weep holes are present with a cavity tray (Figure 33), the likelihood is that the outer leaf is 100 mm brickwork; brick slip systems do not incorporate weep holes.

Figure 33
Weep holes above cavity tray in a conventional masonry wall

Detailing around openings

It should be hard to distinguish brick slips from a standard brick wall if they are laid accurately and have been detailed correctly. A close inspection around openings can often give a strong indication of the form of construction. The presence of PVC-u trims and special profiles not normally seen on door and window frames may hint at the use of brick slips.

Figure 34 shows a window installed into a typical 100 mm brick skin. The window frame abuts the brickwork, and the resulting gap is sealed with mastic. Figure 35, on the other hand, shows a brick slip system being applied. The frame was installed first and brick slips, which overlap the front face of the frame, are being placed afterwards to form a detail similar to a 'check reveal'; in this case, the return edge of the slips is also housed within a channel in a special moulding to form a neat finish.

It is normal practice in some areas (eg Scotland) for check reveals to be constructed (ie window and door frames overlap slightly with the back face of a 100 mm brick outer leaf). This is good practice to provide extra weather resistance in exposed areas. However, in such cases, the inside cheeks of the reveal will be a full half-brick deep, ie 100 mm, and a sub-sill will be required (see below). In Figure 35 the cheeks of the reveal are clearly less than 100 mm, indicating brick slips.

Figure 34
Window reveal of a standard cavity wall

Figure 35
Brick slips overlapping front of a frame (Courtesy of Keskin)

Figure 36
Sub-sills in 100 mm brickwork

With manufactured housing, where both brick slips and the windows are factory-installed, good design of details and the fabrication process allow the slips to be fitted before the frame, thus avoiding an external overlap.

The arrangement of window sills can also provide useful clues. It is difficult to use masonry sub-sills in manufactured housing due to their mass and the problems in fixing them adequately to a volumetric or panellised system. It is most likely that they will be placed on 100 mm brickwork rather than as part of a slip system with some form of framed supporting structure.

Figures 36 and 37 contrast differing sill details with the former having large sub-sills supported on a brickwork skin, whereas the later brick slip system only has the PVC-u window sill.

In addition, with timber-framed construction and a conventional 100 mm brick skin larger movement/compression joints are needed under window sills in order to cope with the shrinkage of the timber with respect to the brick skin. You would expect to find 8 mm joints below sills on the ground floor, with an additional 8 mm if the floor is suspended. On upper floors this requirement increases by an additional 8 mm for each additional floor. If brick slips are used and fixed to the timber frame then these movement joints may be absent although, depending on the construction used, other movement joints (eg at each floor level) may have been introduced.

Figure 37
No sub-sills with brick slip facade

Figure 38
Brick-on-edge sill

Window sills are often produced by the use of bricks on edge, as shown in Figure 38. The fact that on the end bricks of the sill three faces are visible indicates that they are not brick slips. This is reinforced by the full 100 mm cheeks to the reveal.

Another feature of brick-faced concrete panels is the arrangement at the quoins. Figure 39 shows a dwelling made from brick-faced concrete panels. A close inspection of the corners shows that the brickwork is not bonded, but a mitred joint is formed where two panels abut. Another indication is the absence of weep holes.

Figure 39
Brick-faced concrete
panels: inset shows
mitred corner
(Courtesy of Milbank)

Regularity of brickwork

The vertical and horizontal alignment of bricks and their mortar joints, and the regularity of mortar thickness, is dependent on the skill of the person laying them. The production of brick slip panels in a factory environment with grooved fixing panels or insulation boards means that quality control can be rigidly enforced. With brick slips the brickwork appearance should be consistent and regular as can be seen in Figure 40.

Hand-placed brickwork, however, is dependent on the skill of the bricklayer who lays them and the level of quality control on that site. The brickwork in Figure 41 is obviously not a brick slip system due to the poor control of bed and perpend thicknesses.

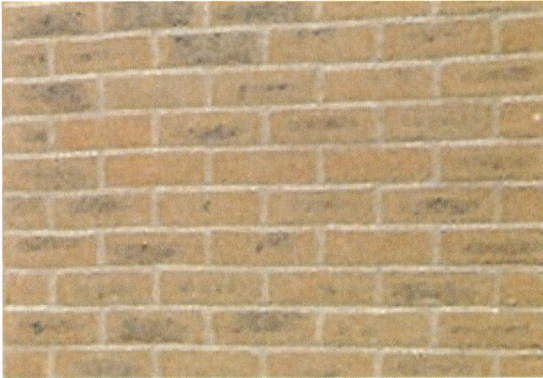

Figure 40
Very regular appearance of a brick slip panel

Figure 41
Hand-laid bricks showing variations in bed and perpend thicknesses

Mortar and brickwork colour banding

A feature of natural materials such as clay bricks is the characteristic variation in shade that usually occurs. In order to avoid colour banding or patching, it is important to ensure that colour blending is undertaken during the manufacturing process and on site. Site practices such as taking bricks from a minimum of three packs at one time and by taking bricks from a top corner and working diagonally towards the opposite bottom corner should ensure a good mix of colour and shade across an elevation. Bricks should not be taken layer by layer, either horizontally or vertically. On larger projects, contractors should receive as many bricks as possible on site at an early stage, to maximise colour consistency throughout the project.

When a development involves manufactured units with factory-applied brick slips it is probable that some slips will need to be fixed on site where two units come together. This increases the probability that differences in colour, both of brick slips and the mortar used to point them, will occur between the factory-fitted and site-applied operations. It is common during the erection of conventional brickwork to produce 'day' work variations with irregular patterns, eg as the quoins are put up first to establish the levels. Variations are most common in the colour of mortar especially when it is mixed on site. Patterns produced are usually horizontal for large areas of brickwork, with triangular areas at corners and adjacent to openings.

With brick slip systems the patterns produced can also be vertical. Figure 42 shows a prefabricated structure being erected on site using brick slips. The unit to the right has already been pointed, whereas on the left the brick slips have yet to be pointed.

Figure 42
Panels of brick slips
in different stages

If a different batch of mortar with a slightly different colour is used then the eye will discern two patches of brickwork of slightly different colours, separated by a vertical line where one area of pointing meets the adjacent one. This effect is illustrated in Figure 43 in Box 2. Four features in the image give clues to the form of construction (in this case volumetric steel with brick slips, partly factory applied, part site applied).

Box 2 External clues to the form of construction

Figure 43
Colour banding in brick slip system

1 The two thick mortar beds show the junction between modules. Thicker than normal joints might be associated with other features such as a cavity tray, but weep holes would be expected above a tray and none is present here.

2 There is a vertical delineation of mortar colour between the two windows — this would not be expected on hand-placed brickwork.

3 The bricks between the two windows are a slightly different shade from the other bricks. Again, a rectangular pattern for shade differences would not be expected on hand-placed brickwork.

4 The mortar used on the right-hand gable is a distinctly different shade to that immediately below. This might happen on a traditional site, but is also entirely consistent with volumetric construction if roof and wall were fabricated at different times.

Damp-proof courses

When framed structures are clad with brick slips the usual arrangement of damp-proof courses (dpcs) found in a conventional 100 mm brick outer leaf is not possible. In some cases, brick slips will stop roughly 150 mm above ground level, with a sheet material (such as cement particle board) being used below, or brick slips may continue to ground level without interruption. In some cases, where the slips continue to ground level, a mastic joint is seen where the dpc might normally be expected. Figure 44 shows a prototype volumetric dwelling using brick slips: no dpc is present. Similarly, other features such as cavity trays will also be absent.

Figure 44
Brick slips without dpc

Thickness of the external wall

Since the 1990s the minimum thickness of a traditional cavity wall has been approx. 265 mm, which represents two skins of masonry with a 50 mm cavity and plastered internal wall. A timber-frame wall will also be around 265 mm thick, represented by 100 mm brick outer leaf, 50 mm cavity, 10 mm sheathing board, 89 mm studs and 12.5 mm plasterboard, giving a total thickness of approx. 261.5 mm). Allowing for variations in cavity width there is not much difference between the two. Thus, any external wall built since then that appears to be finished in brickwork externally, but which is thinner than 265 mm, is probably not of traditional construction.

Steel-frame buildings with storey heights up to 3 m are usually constructed with C section studs at least 75 mm deep. The internal face is then clad with either one or two layers of plasterboard. The external face of the wall will have approx. 70 mm of insulation with either brick slip, brick or some other kind of finish or cladding. The overall thickness could therefore be as low as 200 mm, assuming all of the insulation was on the outside of the steel frame. Figure 45 shows the external wall from a steel-frame dwelling with brick slip external cladding. As can be seen, the total wall thickness is roughly three times the depth of a brick (65 mm), ie approx. 200 mm thick.

Figure 45
External wall of steel frame
building with brick slip exterior

Structural considerations

Examination of the external wall over openings can often give a good indication of construction. A range of lintel designs to support brickwork over openings has been developed; these products are not needed (and in general cannot be fitted) when the building is clad with brick slips. In Figure 46, a parking area is spanned by part of the structure. If the brickwork was a 100 mm outer leaf of cavity construction, a substantial beam would be required to support it. There is no evidence of such a beam; all that is visible is a piece of trim (the black line) masking the edge of the brick slip finish (applied in this case to volumetric steel construction).

Figure 46
Large spans need substantial
support in masonry

Another example is given in Figure 47. The brick face is proud of the render by roughly 20 mm, and the junction between the render and brick finishes is in line with the left-hand side of the window reveal. Such a detail is difficult to construct in conventional masonry, but straightforward if brick slips are used.

Other features point to the use of traditional brickwork, rather than brick slips. Figure 48 shows two features that indicate bricks, rather than brick slips. The first is the brick-on-edge window sill seen previously, and the second is the corbelled detail at eaves level. Both of these features could not easily be reproduced with brick slips.

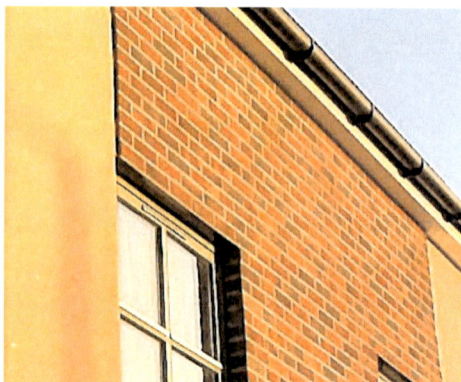

Figure 47
Brick slips and render on thin
joint blockwork

Figure 48
Corbelled brickwork
indicating
conventional
construction

Rendered finish

The use of renders has been common for many years, and in some areas
of the UK, particularly Scotland, is more common than brick. In traditional
masonry construction, renders are normally cement-based and applied
directly to blockwork. Detailing is fairly standardised with the use of bell-
cast and other stop beads where appropriate. Another form of render
system used in refurbishment situations is the type used by the external
wall insulation (EWI) industry. These systems are usually relatively thin
(~ 8 mm) polymer renders applied onto a layer of insulation (typically
40 mm or more thick). Cement-based renders can be used but result in
thicker construction.

Distinguishing between these two types of render system on traditional
masonry construction is straightforward. Tapping the surface (external wall
insulation will sound dull when struck) or inspection at ground level should
be sufficient as can be seen in Figures 49 and 50. The cement render is
approx. 20 mm thick and the render stop bead can be seen, whereas the
external wall insulation system is clearly much thicker than a standard

Figure 49
Cement-based render on masonry

Figure 50
External wall insulation is much thicker than cement render

render. In both cases, the render should stop at the dpc, but a thinner layer of external wall insulation is often applied below dpc to deal with thermal bridging.

Some modern methods of construction can also have a rendered finish that can be either cement render (for example, on a metal lath) or a polymer render incorporating thermal insulation.

The main difference with the use of insulated systems on modern methods of construction occurs when they are applied to framed constructions. On traditional masonry constructions, the insulation is applied directly to the wall surface, whereas on a framed construction, in most cases there will be

Figure 51
External wall insulation applied to a steel-framed building

a drained cavity between insulation and frame. (A drained cavity is a requirement of some, but not all, warranty organisations, and so may not always be present.) Figure 51 illustrates one external wall insulation system applied to a framed construction; note the aluminium stand-off rails used to create the cavity. The cavity needs to drain at the bottom, so look for special trims at that point.

It should be quite easy to distinguish between retrofit external wall insulation and that applied during construction. In a retrofit situation, window sills must be extended to maintain a weather drip after the insulation is applied. This is normally achieved by either extending the integral sill of a window frame (metal profiles are often fixed over the existing sill) or, in the case of brick on edge, the whole sill is clad (Figure 52). In contrast, when applied to a new building, PVC-u profiles can be used to form a much neater finish (Figure 53).

Figure 52
External wall insulation carried over brick-on-edge window sill

Figure 53
Special trims used in
new build situation

Another feature of retro-fit external wall insulation occurs at window jambs
and door frames. The external insulation system frequently overlaps
considerably with the front face of the jamb or frame (Figure 54). Systems
applied during construction should not overlap markedly.

Figure 54
Considerable overlap with
window frame from retro-fit
external wall insulation

Internal inspection

Internal walls

Thickness

Internal walls are usually relatively thin (eg less than 100 mm) unless they are load-bearing, in which case 100 mm blockwork might be used. Occasionally, much thicker walls are found internally. There may be a logical explanation for thicker walls, such as an external wall becoming an internal wall following construction of an extension as in Figure 55, but in other cases there may be no obvious explanation.

One modern method of construction, namely volumetric construction, can lead to thick internal walls. This results when two modules, each manufactured with four walls, are placed next to each other. This is illustrated in Figure 56 which is a plan for volumetric flats.

Figure 55
Thick internal wall resulting from construction of an extension

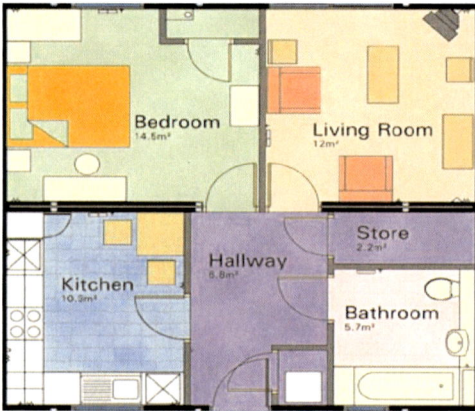

Figure 56
Plan showing double stud wall construction in volumetric flats (Courtesy of Yorkon)

Each flat is made from two modules in volumetric steel, one containing the bedroom and living room, the other the rest of the flat. As can be seen from the plan, the wall separating the living room and store, and the bedroom and kitchen are double thickness. It is unlikely that this would be the case had the flats been designed for conventional or panellised forms of construction.

Wall construction

In general, a plastered finish to walls indicates masonry construction, and that is still the case with modern methods, although some systems (such as Tunnelform) give a solid concrete finish. Tunnelform is normally distinguished from cavity masonry because the open ends of the Tunnelform bays are usually closed with a timber- or steel-frame panel as illustrated in Figure 57 (although they can be closed with masonry).

Lining boards such as plasterboard can be used with almost any construction, from plasterboard on dabs in conventional masonry construction to use on steel- or timber-framed constructions. The use of a stud or cable detector can be informative, but the range of possible constructions is such that it will rarely give a definitive answer. However, plasterboard on dabs can sometimes be indicated using a metal detector because of the absence of fixings.

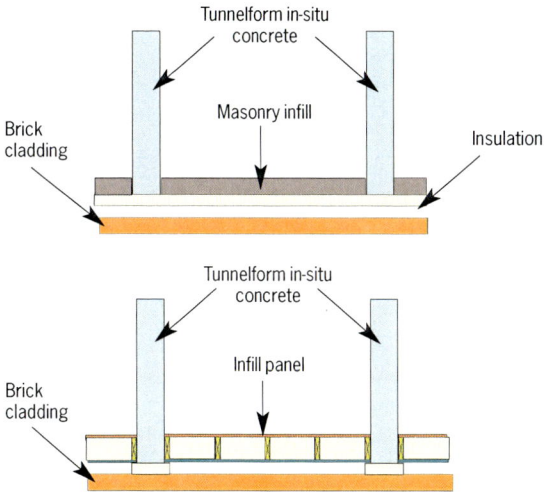

Figure 57
Alternative ways of closing Tunnelform construction

Tapping plasterboard above window openings will sometimes allow timber-frame construction to be distinguished from plasterboard on dabs in masonry construction: in the case of timber-frame construction the plasterboard will be fixed to large timber members forming the lintels, and so sound fairly solid at that point, whereas plasterboard on dabs will sound hollow above the window. There are, though, instances with modern timber-frame where a void is created for services by fixing the plasterboard to battens fixed to the panels. One such system is illustrated in Figure 58.

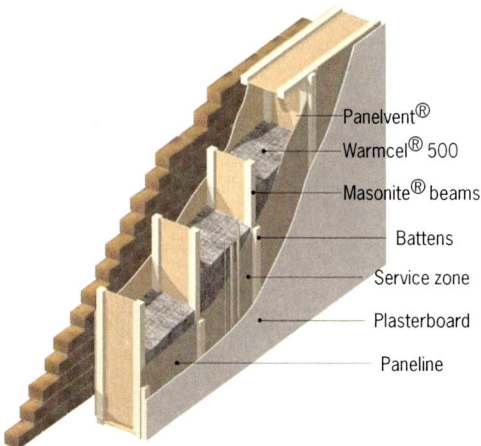

Figure 58
Service zone created by plasterboard on battens (Courtesy of Excel Industries Ltd)

With steel-frame construction, plasterboard is normally fixed directly onto the steel frame so a metal detector should pick that up, although internal lining and partition systems now also use light gauge steel studs (Figure 59). To distinguish between steel-frame construction and a lining system using steel studs, use a metal detector on the inside cheeks of door and window openings: a strong signal indicates steel-frame construction, a weak signal or no signal indicates steel studs for dry lining. With steel-frame construction all internal walls (including load-bearing ones) are usually made from light gauge steel studs. Light gauge steel partitioning systems are not used for load-bearing walls.

A further way of deciding the wall construction is to inspect carefully behind a light switch or similar electrical fitting, remembering to switch off the electricity at the mains first. The material that back boxes are fixed to may be informative, and other clues to the construction may be visible. Figure 60 shows back boxes fixed to galvanised steel in the case of a steel-frame construction.

Figure 59
Modern light gauge steel partitioning system before fixing plasterboard lining

Figure 60
Back boxes fixed to a steel frame

Floors

Ground floor

Ground-floor construction is rarely a good indicator of built form since almost any system can be built on a solid concrete or beam and block floor. An exception is full volumetric construction (in either steel or timber). In this case, a suspended floor is automatically produced by the way volumetric units are assembled. A modern stud detector can be used to distinguish between steel or timber joists. If the ground floor is suspended steel, that is a strong indication of volumetric steel construction.

Intermediate floors

When volumetric buildings are manufactured each module has both a floor and a ceiling. When stacked vertically to form multi-storey structures this leads to the floors between modules having a double layer construction that is considerably deeper than is normally found with a traditional timber floor having 175 mm joists (Figure 61).

Figure 62 shows the junction between two modules before fixing the last piece of plasterboard. A comparison with the depth of the stair riser gives a good indication of scale.

Although technically possible, it is not normal for volumetric construction to be used to create dwellings with large, open spaces. Thus, if the floor construction is much deeper than the unsupported span appears to require, there is a good possibility that volumetric construction has been used, or that the floor may have been upgraded for good acoustic performance.

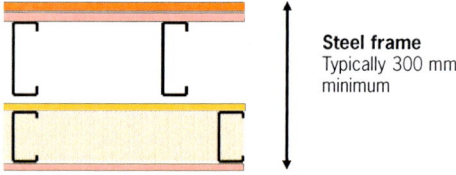

Steel frame
Typically 300 mm
minimum

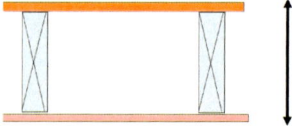

Traditional timber
Typically 200 mm

Figure 61
Comparison of steel
volumetric floor design and
traditional timber

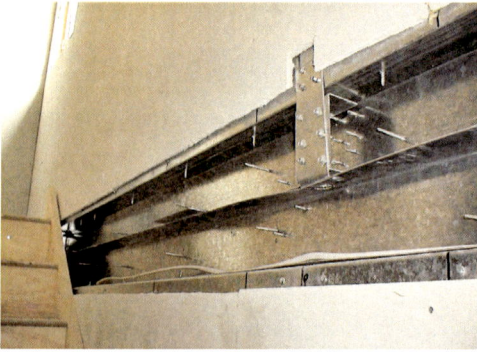

Figure 62
Junction between steel
modules

Another feature of the double-joist construction in volumetric construction is that, depending on the span of the joists, the spacing of the ceiling joists may differ from that of the floor joists above (illustrated in Figure 61). The ceiling joists rarely need to be closer than 600 mm centre to centre, whereas the floor joists are often at 400 mm centres because of the need to support the load. (If using a cable detector to detect steel joists on a ceiling, bear in mind that resilient bars will also give a positive signal.)

Floor cassettes can also give quite deep floors, particularly when timber 'I' beams are used to allow a large span in open-plan locations. The depth of the cassette will depend on the spacing of the joists, the unsupported span, the structural properties of the beams themselves and the load to be carried. However, as an indication, to span up to 6 m with timber I beams at 400 mm centres requires joists to be approx. 350 mm deep.

An indication for the use of floor cassettes is in the use of lifting points. Once installed, the cassettes are usually fully supported around their perimeter so it is normally not practical to lift them by the use of a strap that passes beneath them. Holes are cut in the finished floor surface to create lifting points (Figures 63 and 64), and the hole is sealed up afterwards by fixing a circular plate. Floor cassettes will have these lifting points, but they will not be present in volumetric construction.

A concrete intermediate floor could indicate either masonry construction with concrete planks, or Tunnelform construction which produces concrete intermediate floors. Tunnelform can sometimes be identified by examining the wall construction (see previous section on *Internal walls*).

Figure 63
Lifting point in steel-frame floor cassette

Figure 64
Steel floor cassette being lifted into place

Loft and roof structure

The loft space of a dwelling can often give a good indication of the built form of the rest of the house. It is possible to use most forms of roof construction with any form of superstructure, but there are clues that point to some forms of construction.

Gable and party walls

If the dwelling has gables or party walls it is worth inspecting them from within the loft. If they are boarded this indicates a framed construction and further inspection (fixing methods and use of a cable detector) might give clues to the frame material.

Roof trusses

Roof trusses are as much applicable to dwellings constructed by innovative methods as they are to traditional cavity construction. Trusses are usually of either light gauge steel or timber and can be of conventional design, including attic trusses. Light gauge steel trusses indicate steel-frame construction for the main structure while timber trusses may be used with any construction.

Conventional trusses are not normally boarded so it should be easy to check if the plasterboard for the ceiling below is fixed to the underside of the trusses. If it is not, this indicates volumetric construction.

Lofts suitable for habitation (room-in-the-roof)

In addition to the attic trusses discussed above, another way to make use of the loft space as part of the normal living accommodation, or to design it so that it can be so used at a later date without the need to undertake structural alterations, is to use cassettes to form the floor of the loft and/or the pitched element of the roof. Factory-made floor cassettes are finished with large (2.4 m × 1.2 m) sheets of a flooring grade material rather than standard (2.4 m × 600 mm) flooring chipboard that is normally used for on-site work, and the joists need to be deep enough to accept normal in-use floor loading. The use of cassettes for the pitched elements reduces the need for structural timbers in the loft (purlins and struts) so that a usable open space is created.

The cassettes can be of similar construction to normal wall panels (ie timber-frame, steel-frame or SIP construction). They normally incorporate thermal insulation and are finished internally with a suitable sheet material. In some instances, purlins will be used; if they are, check if the internal sheet material passes behind the purlin (Figures 65 and 66) — if so, a cassette has probably been used.

Aerated concrete plank construction is also highly suited to creating habitable roof spaces.

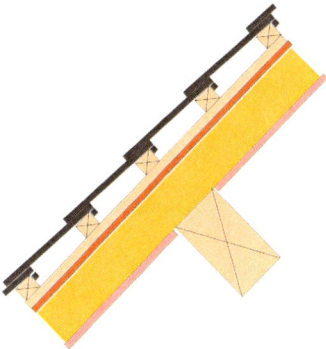

Figure 65
Site-constructed roof: internal lining boards abut purlin

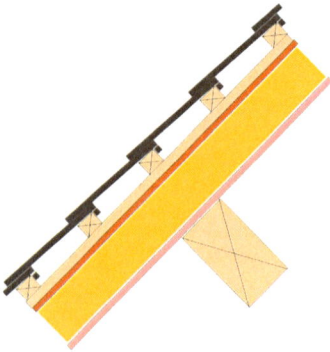

Figure 66
Roof cassette panel: internal lining
boards pass behind purlin

Lofts with attic trusses are usually boarded so it may be difficult to see how the plasterboard of the ceiling below is fixed. However, an access hatch may be provided to get into the void at the eaves or at the ridge. It is unlikely that joists/rafters within these voids will have been fully lined so they should be inspected for clues to the construction of the dwelling.

Another clue is the thickness of the ceiling. With an 8 m span and 40° roof pitch, the timber forming the ceiling joist of an attic truss is roughly 200 mm deep. If used in conjunction with panellised construction, such a truss results in an overall ceiling thickness of around 230 mm. If attic trusses are placed directly on volumetric construction, the overall thickness will probably be higher because of the additional ceiling joists built into the room module beneath. These points are illustrated in Figure 67.

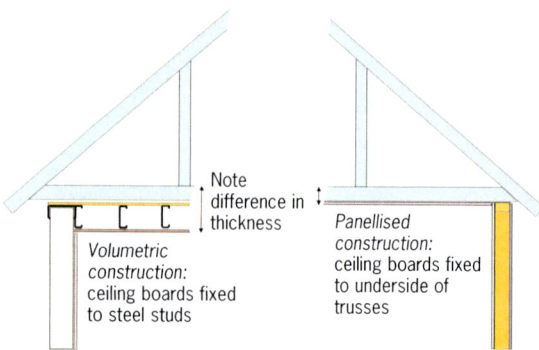

Note
difference in
thickness

*Volumetric
construction:*
ceiling boards fixed
to steel studs

*Panellised
construction:*
ceiling boards fixed
to underside of
trusses

Figure 67
Schematic showing
different ceiling
thicknesses with
volumetric and
panellised
constructions

Site checklist

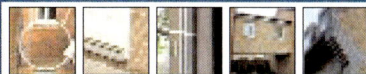

Look out for:
- ☐ Absence of weep holes
- ☐ Unusual detailing around openings
- ☐ *Very* regularly laid out brickwork
- ☐ Unusual day work patterns
- ☐ Absence of damp proof courses or the use of mastic sealants in such places
- ☐ Unusually thin (< 265 mm) external walls
- ☐ Apparently unsupported brickwork

Comments:
Brick slips are most likely to be used on framed constructions, or on solid masonry constructions in combination with other external finishes such as render to create visual variety.

Some brick slip systems incorporate external insulation and are most likely to be used on steel-frame construction.

External wall insulation with render finish (pages 41–44)

Look out for:
- ☐ Thickness of render. Is it > 40 mm?
- ☐ Extended window sills
- ☐ Extent of overlap with door and window frames
- ☐ Drained cavity behind insulation

Comments:
External insulation may have been retro-fitted to an older solid masonry property to improve the thermal performance (compare with neighbouring properties). If used on modern construction it is most likely to be used on steel-frame construction.

Internal inspection of walls (pages 45–48)

Look out for:	Comments:
❑ Thick internal walls	This may result from an external wall becoming an internal wall following construction of an extension, but it can also result from volumetric construction.
❑ Wet-plastered finish to all external walls	This usually indicates traditional construction but can indicate in-situ concrete or concrete panels (decoration may have been applied directly to the concrete).
❑ One form of construction for front and rear walls and a different construction for other walls	This can indicate old cross-wall construction or Tunnelform construction (note: this results in concrete upper floors).
❑ Steel studs in external walls ❑ Steel studs on internal load-bearing walls ❑ Steel on inside cheeks of openings	This can indicate steel-frame construction or an older property dry-lined with a modern steel partitioning system. Steel-frame construction also usually results in all other internal walls (including load-bearing ones) being constructed from steel-frame panels. It is unusual for internal walls to be lined with steel partitioning systems. The presence of steel on the cheeks of openings indicates steel-frame construction.
❑ Timber studs in external walls ❑ Solid-sounding lintel area above openings when struck	Timber studs in external walls indicates timber-frame construction or the presence of dry lining on battens, (often used with panellised systems to create a service zone). If the lintel area is solid when struck the construction is probably timber frame. If in doubt, check behind a light switch (see p 48).

The information in this publication is still correct, it may be out of date or BRE no longer have the expertise to support it. The BRE Group and IHS Markit do not accept any responsibility for any subsequent use of this publication, nor for any errors or omissions they may contain.

Floor construction (pages 49–51)

Look out for:

❏ Steel joists on the ground floor

❏ Steel joists in intermediate floors (use a metal detector on the upper surface of the floor)

❏ Thick floor construction in relation to the span of joists

❏ Lifting points in upper surfaces

Comments:

Steel joists on the ground floor strongly indicates volumetric steel construction. Most other modern methods of construction use a conventional solid or beam and block construction.

This indicates steel-frame construction (either panellised or volumetric). However, check the wall construction as steel floor cassettes are known to have been used with more conventional forms of construction.

This can indicate volumetric construction because of the double-joist construction. It may also indicate engineered joists in conventional construction to allow large spans or incorporation of services.

This indicates the use of floor cassettes.

Loft and roof structure (pages 52–54)

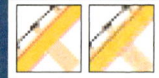

Look out for:	Comments:
❏ Boarded gable or party walls	This indicates framed construction; a metal detector should indicate whether it is steel- or timber-frame.
❏ Rafters boarded on the underside ❏ Absence of struts supporting purlin or no purlin	This indicates roof cassettes if sheet material on the underside of rafters passes over purlins.
❏ Construction of trusses	Steel trusses indicate steel-frame construction; timber trusses can be used with any form of construction.
❏ Fixing of plasterboard to the ceiling below. Is it fixed to trusses?	Fixing of the plasterboard to trusses indicates conventional or panellised construction. If the plasterboard is not fixed to trusses this indicates volumetric construction.

Room-in-the-roof (pages 53–54)

Look out for:

❏ Very thick ceiling/floor constructions with attic trusses

❏ Steel rafters and joists

❏ Construction at eaves

❏ Solid floor

Comments:

This may indicate volumetric construction (ie thickness results from double-joist construction). Use a metal detector on the cheeks of the access way at both ceiling and floor level: a metal joist on the lower half of the floor only, indicates volumetric steel with timber trusses.

These are most likely to be panellised steel construction, especially if the floor is not particularly thick.

If the eaves are accessible via a hatch, check the joist materials.

Tunnelform construction results in a solid floor in a room-in-the-roof.

Further reading

BRE & TRADA. *Multi-storey timber frame buildings: a design guide.* BR 454. Garston, BRE Bookshop, 2003

Harrison H, Mullin S, Reeves B & Stevens A. *Non-traditional houses: identifying non-traditional houses in the UK 1918–75.* BR 469. Garston, BRE Bookshop, 2004

BRE Good Building Guides

56 Off-site construction: an introduction
58 Thin layer mortar masonry
60 Timber frame construction: an introduction

BRE Information Papers

16/01 Prefabricated housing in the UK
       Part 1 A case study: Murray Grove, Hackney
       Part 2 A case study: CASPAR II, Leeds
       Part 3 A summary paper
13/04 An introduction to building with structural insulated panels (SIPs)

BRE CD ROM

AP149 *Non-traditional housing.* A collection of 82 previously published BRE reports and leaflets brought together as pdf files on a CD ROM, eg:
- Falkiner-Nutall steel-framed houses
- Forrester-Marsh houses
- Cast rendered no-fines houses
- Incast houses
- Universal houses
- Fidler houses
- No-fine houses
- BRS type 4 houses
- Nissen-Petren steel-framed houses
- Birmingham Corporation steel-framed houses
- Arrowhead steel-framed houses
- British Housing Steel-framed houses
- Keyhouses Unibuilt steel-framed houses
- Steane steel-framed houses
- Cowieson steel-clad houses